Pretty Theft

by Adam Szymkowicz

A SAMUEL FRENCH ACTING EDITION

SAMUEL FRENCH

FOUNDED 1830

NEW YORK HOLLYWOOD LONDON TORONTO

SAMUELFRENCH.COM

ISBN 978-0-573-69721-0   Printed in U.S.A.   #29146

IMPORTANT BILLING AND CREDIT
REQUIREMENTS

All producers of *PRETTY THEFT* *must* give credit to the Author of the Play in all programs distributed in connection with performances of the Play, and in all instances in which the title of the Play appears for the purposes of advertising, publicizing or otherwise exploiting the Play and/or a production. The name of the Author *must* appear on a separate line on which no other name appears, immediately following the title and *must* appear in size of type not less than fifty percent of the size of the title type.

PRETTY THEFT was produced by Flux Theatre Ensemble at the Access Theatre in New York City, opening on April 24, 2009. The production was directed by Angela Astle, with the following cast and creative team:

MARCO	Todd d'Amour
WAITRESS/BALLERINA	Candice Holdorf
PSYCHIATRIST/BALLERINA	Lynn Kenny
SUZY	Maria Portman Kelly
JOE	Brian Pracht
BOBBY	Zack Robidas
ALLEGRA	Marnie Schulenburg
ALLEGRA'S MOM/SUPERVISOR/BALLERINA	Cotton Wright

Choreographer – Ashley Martinez
Stage Manager – Kate August
Set Design – Heather Cohn
Lighting Design – Andy Fritsch
Sound Design – Kevin Fuller
Costume Design – Becky Kelly
Props Coordinators – Kelly O'Donnell & August Schulenburg
Production Manager – Jason Paradine
Photography & Graphics – Isaiah Tanenbaum
Publicity – Emily Owens, PR

The Flux Theatre Ensemble Core Members are:

August Schulenburg – Artistic Director
Heather Cohn – Managing Director/Development Director
Kelly O'Donnell – Marketing Director
Jason Paradine – Production Manager
Tiffany Clementi – House Manager

Members:

Jake Alexander
Angela Astle
Michael Davis
Candice Holdorf
Christina Shipp
Isaiah Tanenbaum
Cotton Wright

CHARACTERS

ALLEGRA – 18

SUZY – 18

JOE – 20s to 30s

MARCO/ALLEGRA'S FATHER – 30s to 40s

**BALLERINA 2/ALLEGRA'S MOTHER/
SUPERVISOR/PATIENT/ CUSTOMER 2 & 4** – 30s to 50s

**BALLERINA 1/PSYCHIATRIST/PATIENT/
WAITRESS/ CUSTOMER 1 & 3** – 30s to 40s

BOBBY/INTERN/JOE'S FATHER – 20s

NOTE: More Ballerinas are nice but not necessary.

ACKNOWLEDGEMENTS

I would like to thank, in no particular order: Seth Glewen, Emily Owens, Evan Cabnet, Daniella Topol, Moritz von Stuelpnagel, Heather Cohn, Kim Rosenstock and the folks at Ars Nova, Jennie Contuzzi and Epiphany Theatre, the Lark, Heidi Schreck, Chuck Mee and the members of the Joseph Cornell pataphysics class at the Flea, Gary Winter, Joe Kraemer, Richard Feldman, Marsha Norman, Chris Durang, Jim Houghton, The Juilliard School, Stephen Willems, Kristen Palmer, Sharon Steflik, John and Rhoda Szymkowicz, Larry Kunofsky, Chris Snipe, Shawn Helm, Madcap Players, Outsiders Inn Collective, Judy Boals, Patrick Loy, Pat McLaughlin, Frank Basloe, Stephen Gaydos, Stacey Luftig, Devan Sipher, Tish Dace, Megan Smith, Jackson Gay, the many actors who were in readings, workshops or productions of this play, and of course, Angela, Gus and the incredibly talented cast and crew from the Flux Theatre Ensemble production.

– Adam Szymkowicz

For Kristen

*(As the lights rise, two **BALLERINAS** enter and stretch. Perhaps they have been stretching when the audience arrives. Classical music. They begin to dance gracefully.)*

*(**ALLEGRA** enters wearing something inappropriate for a ballerina. She tries to join the **BALLERINAS** but she makes mistakes. The dance continues. **ALLEGRA** goes to make a leap but she lands wrong and falls, hurting her ankle. The **BALLERINAS** continue their dance as **ALLEGRA** eventually gets up and hobbles around. The dance comes to an end and the **BALLERINAS** pull aside the curtain or otherwise reveal the set for Scene One. **ALLEGRA** walks into the scene and sits down.)*

Scene One

(The Group Home.)

*(**SUZY** sits at a table. **ALLEGRA** sits across from her and finishes filling out a form. Their dialogue overlaps slightly at first – neither of them hear the other.)*

ALLEGRA. I'm talking too much, aren't I? I'm sorry about that.

SUZY. It's really cool that you came in.

ALLEGRA. It's just that I feel invisible.

SUZY. I feel like you and I never really got to know each other.

ALLEGRA. Even in my nightmares lately, I'm conspicuously absent. What does it mean when you no longer play a prominent role in your own dreams?

SUZY. I'd be really psyched if, we, like became friends.

ALLEGRA. I guess I'm just not good enough. You know what that's like to never be quite good enough? I should be better. I should be stronger. I just don't know if I can do anything. *(Beat. To* **SUZY**.*)* I can't work here.

SUZY. You totally should work here. That would be cool. I mean, if you want to. Do you want to?

ALLEGRA. I'm just not a very worthwhile human being.

SUZY. *(not listening)* Yeah. You still going out with Bobby?

ALLEGRA. Yeah.

SUZY. He's so cute.

ALLEGRA. Yeah.

SUZY. I just want to tear him apart. Just sink my teeth into that muscular thigh of his, and just tear him into little bits. I just want to gnaw him till there's nothing but bone. I would live on that flesh of his forever, but I mean, you know what that's like. You can do that whenever you want.

ALLEGRA. Is this job hard?

SUZY. It's fine. Especially if you fuck with them. Like the ones who hallucinate. You can pretend like you see shit and then they start to see it. It's a fucking riot.

ALLEGRA. Are they all crazy?

SUZY. Some of them, sure. It's like babysitting and then you go home and you don't have to worry about it cause it's all contained here. Sometimes if I don't like the night girl I get all the clients riled up. I put the two guys together who think they're Jesus and watch them fight about it. And then I just clock out. *(quickly)* Course I wouldn't do that to you.

ALLEGRA. It sounds kind of intimidating.

SUZY. No, it's not. Most of them are afraid anyway. Especially if you say you killed someone or like, I tell them I carry a knife.

ALLEGRA. I should just work at Harry's again.

SUZY. This place is better. I got into UConn because of it. You going to college?

ALLEGRA. Yeah.

SUZY. Which one?

ALLEGRA. Dartmouth.

SUZY. *(unenthusiastic)* Oh.

ALLEGRA. I think I want to study psychology. Be a therapist or something.

SUZY. There's some real nut jobs here.

ALLEGRA. But what if I'm not cut out –

SUZY. It's all instincts.

ALLEGRA. I think my instincts are bad.

(**JOE** *enters carrying an open cardboard box.*)

SUZY. Joe, you're not supposed to be here.

ALLEGRA. Hi.

(**JOE** *stands and stares at the girls.*)

SUZY. Sometimes he doesn't talk. Joe, you're not supposed to be in here. Joe. Joe, go back to where Melody is.

JOE. My box is empty again.

SUZY. I know, Joe. It's just something that happens in the night-time.

JOE. I don't think it should still.

SUZY. You going to say hi to Allegra? She's gonna work here.

ALLEGRA. I'm not sure actually.

SUPERVISOR. *(off)* Joe!

(*As the two girls look towards the voice,* **JOE** *snatches* **ALLEGRA***'s pencil and puts it in his box.*)

JOE. Pretty.

SUZY. *(to Allegra)* So come in at like nine and I'll get Melody to hire you.

Scene Two

(On one side of the stage, **JOE** *is seen in the glow of a TV. Faintly, we can hear what sounds like a ballet.* **JOE** *watches intently. The* **BALLERINAS** *dance around him as he stares at the TV. One* **BALLERINA** *becomes the* **WAITRESS**.*)

(On the other side of the stage, **MARCO** *is at a table in a Diner. The* **WAITRESS** *approaches.)*

WAITRESS. What can I get ya?

MARCO. You here alone?

WAITRESS. Why? You lonely?

MARCO. I'll have some coffee.

WAITRESS. That it?

MARCO. I need to peruse the menu. I want just the right combination. I'm celebrating.

WAITRESS. Yeah?

MARCO. I am, as of this moment, officially retired.

WAITRESS. Aren't you kind of young for that?

MARCO. I'm sick of the game.

WAITRESS. Which game is that?

MARCO. I'm an art dealer.

WAITRESS. No you're not.

MARCO. What do you mean?

WAITRESS. I can tell when someone's lying to me.

MARCO. You ever get sick of it all?

WAITRESS. Yup.

MARCO. I had a good run, though. When I started, Christ, I was a kid. I didn't know anything. Sometimes the best way to learn is to make many very bad mistakes. Don't you think?

WAITRESS. No.

MARCO. I'm going to miss it of course. The adrenaline rush, the danger, the moment you know for sure what you're made of…

WAITRESS. What are you made of?

MARCO. What are you made of?

WAITRESS. I'll come back when you're ready.

Scene Three

(The Group Home. Daytime.)

*(**SUPERVISOR** enters followed by **ALLEGRA**. **JOE** is seated silently holding his box in his hands.)*

SUPERVISOR. We're going to start you off with Joe here. Morning, Joe.

*(**JOE** doesn't respond.)*

SUPERVISOR. He's free to move around as he likes but he spends a lot of his time in this room, I'm afraid. Joe! Joe! Allegra's going to be looking after you today. You hear me Joe? He'll be fine. If you have a problem, just shout. Someone will come eventually.

ALLEGRA. Um…But…

*(Exit **SUPERVISOR**, ignoring **ALLEGRA**. **JOE** watches **ALLEGRA**.)*

ALLEGRA. Hi Joe. Remember me?

JOE. …

ALLEGRA. We met the other day. You like that chair, huh?

JOE. …

ALLEGRA. What do you keep in your box, there Joe?

JOE. …

ALLEGRA. Are you going to just going to stare at me like that?

JOE. …

ALLEGRA. Fine then.

*(**ALLEGRA** sits down. Pulls out a book to read. After a few moments, **JOE** speaks.)*

JOE. Are you or have you ever been a ballerina?

ALLEGRA. *(startled)* I'm sorry?

JOE. Are you or have you ever been a ballerina?

ALLEGRA. I took ballet for a while in middle school.

JOE. OK. What's your favorite color?

ALLEGRA. Purple.

JOE. OK. Do you take any medications?

ALLEGRA. No.

JOE. OK. Is there anything broken at your house that you could bring in that I could fix?

ALLEGRA. I don't think so.

JOE. OK. I like ballerinas. Especially the pink ones.

ALLEGRA. Yes, they're very nice.

JOE. Would you consider yourself a communist, socialist, libertarian, or are you a member of the green party?

ALLEGRA. No.

JOE. OK. Have you spoken to my mother?

ALLEGRA. No. I just started here.

JOE. What do you think she thinks?

ALLEGRA. About what?

JOE. About everything?

ALLEGRA. I don't know Joe. Maybe you should ask her.

JOE. OK. When you were a ballerina did you learn how to leap?

ALLEGRA. I jumped.

JOE. OK. Do you think you could jump higher than my mother?

ALLEGRA. I don't know, Joe.

JOE. OK. Can you jump higher than two meters?

ALLEGRA. I guess.

JOE. Wow! Two meters?

ALLEGRA. Is that high?

JOE. What happened to all the things I collected in my box?

ALLEGRA. I don't know, Joe.

JOE. OK. Are you sure there's nothing broken at your home?

(**JOE** *disappears.* **ALLEGRA** *puts her book down and moves to her* **MOTHER** *in Scene Four.*)

Scene Four

(**ALLEGRA**'s *home.* **ALLEGRA'S MOTHER** *sits watching TV, probably facing away from the audience.*)

ALLEGRA. They all think I'm just wonderful. "You're just wonderful," they said. "You sure you've never done this before?" I must be a natural at seeing problems and helping –

ALLEGRA'S MOTHER. What are you talking about?

ALLEGRA. My first day at work.

ALLEGRA'S MOTHER. Oh. Was that today?

ALLEGRA. They said I was wonderful.

ALLEGRA'S MOTHER. Everyone likes to exaggerate.

ALLEGRA. It's something I'm really good at. Suzy Harris works there. We had lunch together and she gave me pointers.

ALLEGRA'S MOTHER. Isn't she the girl that had that abortion?

ALLEGRA. No.

ALLEGRA'S MOTHER. No? Wasn't that Suzy Harris?

ALLEGRA. *(lying)* That's the other Suzy Harris.

ALLEGRA'S MOTHER. They arrested her for vandalism. It was in the paper.

ALLEGRA. That wasn't her either. The other Suzy Harris gives her a bad name.

ALLEGRA'S MOTHER. …

ALLEGRA. I feel like I'm being shown a new world of people. Like I was put here to understand people's inner workings. And help them.

ALLEGRA'S MOTHER. What are you getting all excited about? Is there some man there?

ALLEGRA. Mom!

ALLEGRA'S MOTHER. Because the worst thing you could do is cheat on Bobby. He's an angel. You'll never find a man like that again. Not one that'll put up with you. God knows it's a cross I must bear.

(pause)

ALLEGRA. She invited me over.

ALLEGRA'S MOTHER. What?

ALLEGRA. I'm going over Suzy's tomorrow.

ALLEGRA'S MOTHER. Don't you usually spent Fridays with Bobby?

ALLEGRA. I can do something else.

ALLEGRA'S MOTHER. Don't take him for granted. You don't give him what he needs and before you know it he'll be chasing anything in a skirt.

ALLEGRA. Why did you say that?

ALLEGRA'S MOTHER. Let me watch the TV.

(They are both quiet for a while.)

ALLEGRA. Suzy wants to go to the hospital with me sometime.

ALLEGRA'S MOTHER. There's no reason. He'll be out soon.

ALLEGRA. He's not coming back.

ALLEGRA'S MOTHER. He'll be out soon.

ALLEGRA. Who said that?

ALLEGRA'S MOTHER. He'll be back here soon. On the couch, making us both miserable.

ALLEGRA. A doctor told you that?

ALLEGRA'S MOTHER. Will you let me watch the TV?! Christ!

*(**ALLEGRA** walks away from her mother. **SUZY** joins her and taking her hand, drags her into Scene Five.)*

Scene Five

(The Health and Beauty Aid section of a Pharmacy.)

SUZY. This is where I go for all my beauty needs. It may not be the best stuff, but you can't beat the price.

ALLEGRA. It's cheaper at Rite Aid.

SUZY. *(trying on a lipstick)* I get incredible discounts. What do you think of this one?

ALLEGRA. It's good.

SUZY. Is it provocative?

ALLEGRA. Somewhat.

SUZY. Is it tarty enough? Would the cops stop me in this lipstick? That's what I want to know.

ALLEGRA. I think it's stronger than a slut but not quite a whore. A harlot?

SUZY. Perfect. Harlot red. (SUZY *puts the lipstick in her bag.)*

(pause)

ALLEGRA. I used to want to be your friend.

SUZY. What?

ALLEGRA. In like the sixth grade.

SUZY. You would have been the only one.

ALLEGRA. No. All the attention you got…

SUZY. *(putting other items in her bag)* Well I wouldn't shut up, would I? When you don't shut up, the boys notice you. Course, eventually you realize no one was really listening. And you stop speaking up in class – realize maybe you weren't saying anything anyway – not something someone else couldn't say better – usually a boy. And the boys who seemed to be listening to you weren't quite the right boys.

ALLEGRA. Sometimes I wanted to hit you.

SUZY. *(stuffing her pockets)* So you stopped talking. But then you realize if you lift up your shirt there are boys that like that too. But maybe those aren't quite the right boys either because then later those boys want to see what's in your pants. And want to put themselves in you even if you're not ready and maybe those aren't the right boys either but at least they need you for a few minutes.

ALLEGRA. And you wore those skirts.

SUZY. *(stuffing her bag)* Then you go after your friend's boyfriend because it's wrong and it's fun and because your friend is pretty. And you get him but once you have him, you realize he's no good. And your friend hates you. But you do it again anyway to another friend. And the girls all begin to hate you. They call you a skank and they call you a whore. But some of the boys like you some of the time. But they think you're a slut. So you embrace it because what else can you do? You buy a t-shirt that says "Fuckdoll" and a series of short skirts and you try on provocative lipsticks.

ALLEGRA. Help me pick out a provocative lipstick.

(**SUZY** *selects a lipstick for* **ALLEGRA**. *Then* **SUZY** *empties the whole shelf into her bag.*)

(**ALLEGRA** *leaves* **SUZY** *and walks into Scene Six while putting on her new lipstick.*)

Scene Six

(The Group Home.)

*(**JOE** is humming one long note over and over and rocking on his feet, back and forth. **ALLEGRA** watches him.*

*(Enter **SUZY**.)*

SUZY. Hey.

ALLEGRA. Hey.

SUZY. They want you in the kitchen. They're going to *train* you.

ALLEGRA. Oh.

SUZY. I'll watch him.

ALLEGRA. *(rushing out)* Thanks.

SUZY. *(shouting after her)* Love the lipstick.

ALLEGRA. *(off)* Thanks.

SUZY. So you're humming today.

*(**JOE** continues to hum.)*

SUZY. I hate it when you do that.

*(**JOE** continues to hum.)*

SUZY. Stop humming.

*(**JOE** continues to hum.)*

SUZY. I bet if Allegra told you to stop, you would. She likes you, you know.

*(**JOE** stops humming and looks at **SUZY**.)*

SUZY. She said to me just yesterday, she said, "I like Joe. I think I'll purchase a new lipstick so that he will see it on me and like me all the more." "There's something about Joe," she said later. "There's something about him that's different from other boys, even my current boy-toy, Bobby." You should try to kiss her. That's what girls like.

JOE. I'm going to get a plant.

SUZY. Did you hear what I said, Joe?

JOE. What?

SUZY. Allegra likes you.

JOE. We have a professional relationship. I am a client and she is part of the staff.

SUZY. Have you ever had a girlfriend?

(**JOE** *starts humming again.*)

SUZY. If you had a girlfriend you would know that girls want you to kiss them. Allegra especially. She told me.

JOE. She told you?

SUZY. Yeah.

JOE. She's a member of the staff.

SUZY. Have you ever had a kiss, Joe?

(**JOE** *begins to hum.*)

SUZY. Do you know how? You want to do it right for Allegra, don't you? Stop humming.

(**JOE** *stops humming.*)

SUZY. Close your eyes. Put your lips together.

(**SUZY** *kisses him. A long and powerful kiss.* **SUZY** *stumbles away from it and sits down. She is shaken.*)

SUZY. That was good.

(**JOE** *begins humming again. He looks down at his box as though it may have collected the kiss. He starts rocking his body back and forth. He stands and rocks forwards and backwards in big jerky movements.* **ALLEGRA** *returns.*)

ALLEGRA. Hey. You OK?

SUZY. Yeah.

(**SUZY** *stands and drops a barrette into* **JOE***'s box.*)

SUZY. *(exiting)* See you later.

ALLEGRA. Joe, are you upset or something?

(**JOE** *doesn't respond.*)

(**ALLEGRA** *watches him for a minute then picks up her book to read.*)

(a long silence)

JOE. There are things that are untouchable aren't there?

ALLEGRA. What?

JOE. Like a ballerina while she is spinning. You can't touch her.

ALLEGRA. I guess.

JOE. *(stops rocking)* Ballerinas are pretty, aren't they? Aren't they, Allegra?

ALLEGRA. Yes. Except the ugly ones.

JOE. The professional ones have to be pretty. Right Allegra? Or else no one would pay to see them.

ALLEGRA. Sure.

JOE. *(trying a new tact)* What did you have for breakfast today?

ALLEGRA. I didn't have breakfast.

JOE. OK. You should always have breakfast. I had a banana and some oatmeal. That sounds like a good breakfast, doesn't it? Doesn't it?

ALLEGRA. Uh huh.

JOE. What did your mother have for breakfast today?

ALLEGRA. I don't know, Joe.

JOE. OK. What do you think my mother had for breakfast today?

ALLEGRA. I've never met your mother, Joe.

JOE. But what do you think she had?

ALLEGRA. I don't know.

JOE. *(thinks)* I think she had a banana and some oatmeal. Do you think she likes raisins in her oatmeal?

ALLEGRA. Hard to say, Joe.

JOE. I think she probably does because I like raisins and we are partially made of the same genetic material.

*(**SUPERVISOR** enters.)*

SUPERVISOR. How's everything in here?

ALLEGRA. Fine.

SUPERVISOR. What are you doing, Joe?

(**JOE** *doesn't respond.*)

ALLEGRA. He's been very talkative.

SUPERVISOR. Joe, I was wondering if you could fix the TV like you did before. Remember what you did last time? Well it's gone all fuzzy again. Joe? Joe? You think you could do that for me?

ALLEGRA. Joe?

JOE. What?

ALLEGRA. Will you please fix the TV?

JOE. OK.

(**JOE** *exits to fix the TV.*)

SUPERVISOR. *(following* **JOE** *out)* *(a warning)* He seems quite taken with you.

ALLEGRA. I'm working on my people skills.

(**ALLEGRA** *goes back to her book. A moment.* **JOE** *re-enters and snatches* **ALLEGRA** *'s bookmark without her noticing.* **ALLEGRA** *continues to read.* **SUZY** *enters.*)

SUZY. So I was thinking we could go see that movie. Just you and me. What's it called? Ben Affleck's in it.

ALLEGRA. *(looking up)* We're going to the hospital today.

SUZY. Oh.

ALLEGRA. What?

SUZY. I forgot about that.

ALLEGRA. Maybe we could still see the movie after.

SUZY. Yeah, I guess.

(silence)

ALLEGRA. What happened this morning with Pat?

SUZY. She threw her cup at me. She's getting an assessment for it.

ALLEGRA. Finally.

(**BOBBY** *enters.*)

BOBBY. Hey. You ready?

ALLEGRA. Oh.

SUZY. Hi Bobby.

ALLEGRA. You're not supposed to be here today.

BOBBY. Whatever. I don't care. You and me are gonna go see that new movie with Ben Affleck.

ALLEGRA. Suzy and I are going to the hospital.

BOBBY. No, no, no. Go another day.

ALLEGRA. But Suzy and I had it planned.

SUZY. Yeah, I don't think I really want to go.

ALLEGRA. Oh.

SUZY. To the hospital.

ALLEGRA. Oh. But you said…

SUZY. Sometimes I get caught up in the moment. Sorry.

ALLEGRA. Oh. OK.

SUZY. Sorry.

BOBBY. All right. So get your stuff.

ALLEGRA. No. I'm going to the hospital.

BOBBY. I'm not dropping you off.

ALLEGRA. I'll call a car.

BOBBY. Come on. I already bought the tickets.

SUZY. I'll go with you.

ALLEGRA. You already bought the tickets?

BOBBY. I'm gonna buy them. Get your stuff.

ALLEGRA. No.

BOBBY. Well, fuck you then.

ALLEGRA. You're an asshole. You know that?

SUZY. I'll go with you.

BOBBY. *(looks her over)* Yeah. All right.

SUZY. Cool. Can we get popcorn?

BOBBY. Yeah, all right.

ALLEGRA. Wait.

BOBBY. What?

ALLEGRA. Nothin'. Never mind. Go.

BOBBY. *(mumbling)* Crazy fucking…

    (**BOBBY** *and* **SUZY** *exit.* **ALLEGRA** *watches them go.)*

    *(***JOE*** *reenters.)*

JOE. I fixed it. Allegra, I fixed it.

ALLEGRA. He's an asshole anyway, isn't he?

JOE. OK. Did you want to see the TV I fixed?

ALLEGRA. Not now, Joe.

JOE. OK.

ALLEGRA. But he has to put up with me too.

JOE. OK. *(looking at his watch)* Your shift was over three minutes ago.

ALLEGRA. Yeah.

JOE. You can stay here with me. I won't tell.

ALLEGRA. It's not like I'm Suzy and can get whoever I want.

JOE. You were seven minutes late this morning. You can get in trouble for that. The present administration does not look too fondly on tardiness.

ALLEGRA. Why don't I have that?

JOE. Plus I have to wait seven minutes for you. Maybe tomorrow eight or nine or who knows.

ALLEGRA. I'll see you later

JOE. You have to come in at nine a.m.

ALLEGRA. Uh huh.

JOE. You should come on time. Allegra?

ALLEGRA. What?

JOE. I'm very smart you know, Allegra, and I'm very strong.

ALLEGRA. *(as she exits)* Uh huh.

Scene Seven

(**BALLERINAS** *wheel out a TV and* **JOE** *sits in front of it and begins to watch more ballet.*)

(*On the other side of the stage,* **MARCO** *and the* **WAITRESS** *in the diner.* **MARCO** *sits at a table drinking coffee.* **WAITRESS** *approaches him.*)

WAITRESS. More coffee?

MARCO. How many's that been?

WAITRESS. My guess between eight and twelve.

MARCO. It's too many, don't you think?

WAITRESS. So you don't want more?

MARCO. Is it always this empty?

WAITRESS. There ain't nothing here. People only come here by accident.

MARCO. I came here on purpose.

WAITRESS. Really?

MARCO. To get away.

WAITRESS. Oh. But how'd you know it was here?

MARCO. I came here by accident once.

WAITRESS. That's what I'm saying.

(*pause*)

MARCO. Let me ask you something, you ever been kidnapped, held hostage, anything like that?

WAITRESS. Why, you want to take me away from this hell hole?

MARCO. Just wondering.

WAITRESS. You say the word and I'll up and pack. Don't have to point a gun or nothing.

MARCO. You're just looking for an excuse.

WAITRESS. We're all looking for an excuse.

MARCO. I will have another cup.

WAITRESS. It's your body.

MARCO. Nothing's mine.

(pause)

WAITRESS. I never been kidnapped. But I saw a man get shot once. A stranger too. You be careful here.

MARCO. You're here to protect me.

WAITRESS. If you're that kind of man, there's no way I'm going anywhere with you.

MARCO. What kind's that?

WAITRESS. A mama's boy. You especially close to old women, hide in their skirts?

MARCO. I like young girls, actually.

WAITRESS. *(laughing)* I don't want to know about that.

Scene Eight

(The Movie Theater.)

*(***SUZY*** *and* ***BOBBY*** *sit, the glow of the screen on their faces.)*

SUZY. Allegra says you're going to UConn in the fall. I am too! Isn't that great?! We could even have some of the same classes.

BOBBY. Shut up. I want to see this.

SUZY. It's just the previews. That's gotta be rough though – you going to one school and Allegra going to another. Something like that really takes a toll on a relationship. No matter how strong it is. Because you have separate experiences and you know a lot of girls are going to be paying attention to you. Like more than in high school. And that's hard on a relationship.

BOBBY. You done?

SUZY. I know a lot of couples who broke up because –

BOBBY. Listen, I didn't know you were going to talk the whole time. I wouldn't have asked you to come.

SUZY. I'll be quiet. *(after a pause)* You don't think I'm a bad person, do you?

Scene Nine

(On the other side of the stage.)

(In **JOE***'s room.* **JOE** *is asleep in bed. The* **BALLERI-NAS** *dance around* **JOE***'s bed. The music swells. They lift* **JOE***'s box in the air and dance with it. One of the* **BALLERINAS** *becomes the* **SUPERVISOR***. She speaks to the audience.)*

SUPERVISOR. *(as she takes objects out of* **JOE***'s box)* We no longer wonder where the pens go, the pads, the rubber bands, the paper clips and Mrs. Thompson's dentures. All of us know they're in Joe's box. When he first came here, we tried to get him to give back his pilfered items. But that was a disaster.

It's the only thing that upsets him. If he doesn't see you, he doesn't care, but if he does, he screams and cannot be consoled. So it was just easier to let him keep things until the night-time. Even Evelyn's phone. Because it's just easier. I have a home, a husband a kid. I don't need any more screaming in my day than I already have. So we let him keep whatever he gets in his hands. Until the night when he's completely knocked out and I take it all back.

Once I found a pair of women's underwear in the box. I suspect Suzy. But I can't accuse her and I've learned not to ask him about things in the box. He won't speak of them, won't let you touch them. The only thing I leave in the box, is his ballerina doll. A gift from the former supervisor, now deceased. He likes it. I've always felt there's no harm in it. I've always felt there's no harm in him. His mother disagrees.

Scene Ten

(The Movie Theatre.)

*(***SUZY*** and ***BOBBY*** *stare at the screen.)*

BOBBY. This sucks.

SUZY. I liked the last one he was in.

BOBBY. Huh?

SUZY. Bobby, what do you look for in a girl?

BOBBY. I don't know. What kind of question's that?

SUZY. How did you decide on Allegra?

BOBBY. What do you care?

SUZY. Is it her lips?

BOBBY. I don't know.

SUZY. Do her lips taste good?

BOBBY. I guess.

SUZY. Is it her breasts?

BOBBY. What?

SUZY. She's sexy.

BOBBY. I guess.

SUZY. Do you think I'm sexy?

BOBBY. You're OK.

SUZY. Do you wish you could touch me? Just reach out and touch any part of me like it belonged to you? You're the kind of person who takes what he wants, aren't you?

BOBBY. I dunno.

SUZY. I think you are. I like that very much.

BOBBY. This movie sucks. Let's go.

SUZY. It's a shame to waste the dark.

BOBBY. Huh?

SUZY. You can kiss me, if you want.

BOBBY. You trying to get me in trouble with Allegra?

SUZY. I won't tell.

BOBBY. Aren't you her friend?

SUZY. I want to be your friend too.

BOBBY. I got friends.

SUZY. You have friends you kiss in the dark when no one's looking?

BOBBY. I could have those if I wanted them.

SUZY. I bet you could.

BOBBY. If I kissed you, you'd never be the same. My kiss is devastating.

SUZY. I don't believe you.

BOBBY. Dude, what did I just say?

Scene Eleven

...at was **JOE**'s *bedroom is now a hospital room.*
ALLEGRA *at a bed talking to her* **FATHER** *who faces away from us. He wears an oxygen mask and does not move. He is unconscious.*)

ALLEGRA. And I'm working at this like group home with Suzy Harris. We hang out a lot. You know who she is? I think you'd like her. She's a lot of fun. She was supposed to come here with me today but...she couldn't make it.

Bobby's good. He works at the garden place in Salem sometimes on the weekends. He wishes he could be here too. He's uh...a good boyfriend. I think it'll last for us. One of the great...things.

Fuck! It's just as hard to talk to you now that you can't talk back. I can't ever say the right thing to you. You're just so...not there, aren't you. You always ignore me. I know even if you can hear me right now, you're not paying attention. You never...Why don't I matter to you? What do you want from me?!! Maybe you just want to be left alone.

Well, that's what I'll do then. I'm sorry I disturbed your death bed you selfish fucking bastard! You self-centered, egotistical, pompous, fucking, bastard! I don't care what you want! I hope you die! I hope you fucking die real soon! You can fucking rot and be eaten by worms! I hope fucking worms eat you! Worms with big fucking teeth! And rats and flies and vultures! I hope vultures dig you up and take you out of the casket, and fly away with you! You fuck!

(pause)

I miss you.

I've always missed you. I'm sorry. I don't want you to die. I'm sorry. I'm sorry. Oh, Christ, I'm so sorry. Please don't die. You're so small. Please, Daddy.

*(***ALLEGRA*** kisses his forehead.)*

Scene Twelve

(The Movie Theatre.)

BOBBY. A kiss from me would ruin a girl like you.

SUZY. Oh God. Never mind. Never mind. Let's just watch the movie.

*(**BOBBY** and **SUZY** stare at the screen for a minute. Then **BOBBY** leans over and kisses her. They start making out – really going at it. They break.)*

SUZY. Did someone tell you you were a good kisser?

BOBBY. What do you mean?

SUZY. You're kind of bad. You can't just stick your tongue in and not move it.

BOBBY. You have to let the experience wash over you.

SUZY. It's not my fault you're a bad kisser.

BOBBY. I am not a bad kisser. You wiggle too much.

*(**BOBBY** grabs her and kisses her again. She kisses back. They break.)*

SUZY. That was a little better.

BOBBY. A little? Damn, woman. I can't believe I'm wasting this talent on you.

SUZY. I hope that's not your only talent.

BOBBY. Every girl I've ever kissed said I was the best kisser.

SUZY. They were lying to you. I'm sorry but you are really bad at that. Maybe with time, and practice…In any case I wouldn't go around bragging about it. It tends to raise expectations and that's exactly what you don't want. Maybe you should practice on some inanimate objects before you get into a spin the bottle game or something in college. Whatever you do, don't let go of Allegra. Any girl that lets you kiss her is a keeper.

*(**BOBBY** kisses her again. This time it's more intense. They break. **BOBBY** waits for her reaction.)*

SUZY. Yeah, I mean that was OK.

BOBBY. *(getting up)* This is bullshit.

SUZY. *(following him out)* Wait for me. I still need a ride. Hey, mush-mouth. Wait for me.

Scene Thirteen

(The Group Home.)

(JOE is staring at ALLEGRA who tries to read. After a while, she drops the book, distracted.)

JOE. You were early today. Almost ten minutes early. Did you get up earlier? Allegra? Did you get up earlier?

ALLEGRA. I dunno. I didn't sleep.

JOE. You should always sleep. I always go to sleep at eight and wake up at five. Do you think my mother gets up at five?

ALLEGRA. How come you treat me different than the other girls?

JOE. …

ALLEGRA. Like you pretend you can't hear them if you don't want to do what they say.

(pause)

JOE. Well, you were a ballerina so you're different.

ALLEGRA. But I'm not a ballerina.

JOE. I think you're a ballerina.

ALLEGRA. What does that have to do with anything?

JOE. Don't yell at me.

ALLEGRA. *(louder)* I'm not yelling at you.

JOE. OK.

ALLEGRA. You'd do whatever I told you, wouldn't you?

JOE. OK.

ALLEGRA. Stand on one foot.

(JOE looks at her.)

(JOE stands on one foot.)

ALLEGRA. Get on all fours.

(He does.)

ALLEGRA. Tell me a secret.

JOE. *(thinks)* Sometimes I don't get up until five thirty a.m.

ALLEGRA. Never mind.

(JOE *stays on all fours. Seeing that* JOE *isn't getting up,* ALLEGRA *sits on his back. She sighs. Stares off numbly.*)

ALLEGRA. My father died last night.

JOE. OK. *(long pause)* My father died too.

ALLEGRA. Oh.

JOE. Before I came here.

ALLEGRA. Oh.

JOE. He was tall.

ALLEGRA. My father was too.

JOE. OK. They say I look like my father. But only sometimes.

ALLEGRA. They say I look like my father.

JOE. OK. Who?

ALLEGRA. People.

JOE. OK.

(BOBBY *enters.* ALLEGRA *gets off* JOE*'s back.*)

BOBBY. Hey.

JOE. *(from the ground)* You're early. He's early.

ALLEGRA. I'm so glad you're here.

(ALLEGRA *goes to hug* BOBBY. BOBBY *doesn't hug back as much as he could.*)

BOBBY. *(breaking the hug)* Listen we gotta talk.

ALLEGRA. Thank God. I need someone to talk to.

BOBBY. Not in front of the retard.

ALLEGRA. He's not...Joe, will you go find Melody please.

(JOE *gets up and exits.*)

BOBBY. It's just...

ALLEGRA. The funeral's tomorrow.

BOBBY. We'll be going to different schools.

ALLEGRA. What?

BOBBY. I don't know. Maybe it's not such a good idea.

ALLEGRA. What's not a good idea?

BOBBY. Us staying together.

ALLEGRA. You just thought of this?

BOBBY. Yeah.

ALLEGRA. Today?

BOBBY. You always want me to tell you how I feel. These are my feelings. Don't you want to hear about them?

ALLEGRA. Your feelings?

BOBBY. Yeah.

ALLEGRA. What feelings?

BOBBY. Well, you know. I been thinking.

ALLEGRA. You don't love me. I'm no good.

BOBBY. No, it's just…

ALLEGRA. You don't want me.

BOBBY. No, it's not that. It's just…We're young. I want to fuck other girls. I want to be free to do that at school. There's lots of different kinds of girls out there and most of them I've never even kissed. I'm sorry. Now you're mad at me.

ALLEGRA. What are you talking about?

BOBBY. You know, girls with longer legs, or bigger breasts. Blondes, brunettes, redheads, like girls who play field hockey. Um, girls who wear those shirts that show their stomachs, uh…girls –

ALLEGRA. So we're taking a break?

BOBBY. Yeah, you can call it that if you want. I just really need to experience lots of stuff you know, like other girls. Hopefully lots of other girls. You know, while I'm still attractive.

ALLEGRA. Wow.

BOBBY. Yeah.

ALLEGRA. I can't believe you.

BOBBY. I can be pretty unbelievable.

ALLEGRA. You…You're a fucker!

BOBBY. I thought you'd be mad.

ALLEGRA. Get out of here!

BOBBY. I can still give you a ride.

ALLEGRA. I don't want a fucking ride. You fucking cocksucker. Get the fuck out of here!

BOBBY. Whoa there.   ·

ALLEGRA. Get out! Get out!

BOBBY. You don't have to be so angry. Is this about your dad, cause I'm sorry that he's dead and everything.

ALLEGRA. *(picking up objects and throwing them at him)* Get! Out! Get! Out!

BOBBY. Fucking nutjob. You belong here!

(**BOBBY** *exits.*)

(**ALLEGRA** *collapses in a chair. After a while,* **JOE** *returns.*)

JOE. He was early.

ALLEGRA. Come here. *(He does.)* Hold me.

(**JOE** *holds her.* **ALLEGRA** *sobs.*)

JOE. Your shift is over in two minutes.

ALLEGRA. Hold me tighter.

JOE. Is that man your boyfriend?

(**ALLEGRA** *sobs louder.*)

JOE. I'm going to buy a cactus for my birthday. Cause I should have a plant. Everyone should have a plant, don't you think, Allegra?

ALLEGRA. *(between sobs)* Uh huh.

JOE. I'm going to order it through the mail so I have something.

(**ALLEGRA** *sobs.*)

JOE. I want something of my own that won't disappear at night. Something alive.

(**ALLEGRA** *sobs.*)

ALLEGRA. Hold me tighter.

JOE. OK. I'm strong.

ALLEGRA. Ow. *(He lets go.)* Tighter. Hold me 'til I don't know who I am.

JOE. I know who you are.

ALLEGRA. You do, don't you.

> (**ALLEGRA** *looks at him.* **ALLEGRA** *kisses him. He kisses back. He holds her tightly. Suddenly,* **ALLEGRA** *screams.*)

ALLEGRA. Get away. Get away from me! Don't touch me! Get your hands off me!

> (*The* **SUPERVISOR** *and* **SUZY** *run in to see* **ALLEGRA** *hitting* **JOE** *who is trying to hold her.* **ALLEGRA** *frees herself and runs from the room.* **JOE** *watches her go.*)

JOE. I may have held her too tightly.

Scene Fourteen

(On one side of the stage, the TV is on but **JOE** *is not there to watch it.)*

(On the other side of the stage, The Diner. **MARCO** *sits. The* **WAITRESS** *stands talking to him.)*

MARCO. I have made a great deal of money and almost none of it legally. Does that shock you?

WAITRESS. Not really.

MARCO. I'm not a good person. I was once maybe for a short few years. Until I discovered what I was good at.

WAITRESS. And what's that?

MARCO. Deception. Thievery.

WAITRESS. What do you steal?

MARCO. It's not important.

WAITRESS. Can I guess?

MARCO. No.

WAITRESS. Are you a jewel thief?

MARCO. Yes. You got it in one.

WAITRESS. Asshole. Tell me.

MARCO. Let's just say if caught I would be put away for a very long time.

WAITRESS. How do you know I won't turn you in?

MARCO. I'm entertaining.

WAITRESS. You're helping to pass the time.

MARCO. Is that all?

WAITRESS. How do you do it?

MARCO. What?

WAITRESS. Steal things.

MARCO. Well, I guess there's no harm in sharing a few secrets.

*(**MARCO** gestures for her to sit. She does.)*

MARCO. *(cont.)* The first thing is you got to be invisible. You have to look like everyone else. Change your appearance often. Be unmemorable.

WAITRESS. I think I'll remember you.

*(The **SUPERVISOR** shuts off the TV.)*

Scene Fifteen

(**SUZY** *and* **ALLEGRA** *at the Pharmacy.* **SUZY** *shoplifts.*)

ALLEGRA. I just can't go back there.

SUZY. I'll borrow my mom's car. We'll take a trip. The rest of the summer we'll just drive. See the country like Jack Kerouac. Anyway that job sucks and they underpay and overwork.

ALLEGRA. Why didn't you tell me that when I applied for the job?

SUZY. Cuz I wanted you to work there.

ALLEGRA. There's a funeral.

SUZY. You want to go to the funeral?

ALLEGRA. No.

SUZY. So let's just go.

ALLEGRA. Yeah, right? He's fucking dead. What does he care?

SUZY. When are you going to get a chance like this to just take a trip? Anyway I got to get out of here. Your fucking boyfriend keeps calling me.

ALLEGRA. He's not my boyfriend. He's calling you?

SUZY. Yeah I gave him my number but I didn't think he'd call.

ALLEGRA. You talk to him?

SUZY. No. I'm going cross-country with you.

ALLEGRA. Yeah, good, all right, yeah.

(**ALLEGRA** *picks up a suitcase and walks into Scene Sixteen.*)

Scene Sixteen

44

(ALLEGRA's house. ALLEGRA'S MOM sits, fa
from us, watching TV. ALLEGRA approaches he

ALLEGRA. I know you're probably mad at me for leaving before the funeral, but I just can't do it. My whole body itches and it won't stop until I get in a car and can't see this house or this town or this state from the rearview window.

This way is better. This way I'll come back from my trip and go straight to school and you won't have to look at me or think about me. You can tell people you have a daughter but you won't have to talk to me on the phone or see me on the couch. I'll be a no-maintenance daughter just like you always wanted.

I'm going to go now. I know someday you'll want to talk to me again. Maybe after I graduate and get a job and get married and buy a house and have my own daughter. Then you can talk to her and be her favorite and then we can pretend you were a really great mother. She won't know and I don't have to tell her.

But now I'm going to get on the road and push you out of my mind and I probably won't think of you until I get to the Grand Canyon or some other fairly good canyon and maybe I'll cry in front of the mammoth orange hole in the ground or maybe I'll smile because it's so beautiful and I'm free and windswept.

But first I'm going to get into Suzy's mom's car and we'll drive till there's just drops left in the tank and as we cross the border into Massachusetts, we'll roll into the first gas station where I'll get some Ding Dongs and some orange soda and I'll bite into the first one sitting on the hood, watching the car slurp up gas. Then I'll get in the driver's seat and put my foot on the accelerator until I can't keep my eyes open anymore. So I pull over and we both close our eyes and sleep until we're awoken at three am by separate but equally terrible nightmares.

Scene Seventeen

(*The Group Home.*)

(**PSYCHIATRIST** *holding clipboard, talking with* **SUPERVISOR**)

PSYCHIATRIST. I also want to talk to the other girl who was alone with him that day.

SUPERVISOR. Neither of them are returning my calls and they won't come into work. They're kids you know? Something like this scares them.

PSYCHIATRIST. (*writing on her clipboard*) Does this kind of thing happen often here?

SUPERVISOR. No, no. What are you writing? You're not here to assess me.

PSYCHIATRIST. I'm just trying to get the whole picture.

SUPERVISOR. I'm not hiding anything.

PSYCHIATRIST. If you often have a sexually charged atmosphere…

SUPERVISOR. Who said that? No one said that.

PSYCHIATRIST. I really should talk to those girls.

SUPERVISOR. You and me both.

PSYCHIATRIST. Where's Joseph?

SUPERVISOR. They're getting him. I think you'll find this is an isolated incident. We don't have problems with him.

PSYCHIATRIST. Don't talk to me like that.

SUPERVISOR. Like what?

(**INTERN** *leads* **JOE** *in.* **JOE** *still has his box.*)

SUPERVISOR. Hi, Joe. This woman wants to talk to you for a minute. OK? OK, Joe? Joe, you hear me?

PSYCHIATRIST. Joe, my name is Nancy. I want to talk to you for a minute. Joe, you think you could answer some questions for me? (*goes to his box and looks inside*) What's this?

SUPERVISOR. You shouldn't…

(**PSYCHIATRIST** *takes out the ballerina.*)

(**JOE** *begins to scream extremely loudly. He begins to hit himself in the head. He lashes out at the* **PSYCHIATRIST**, *trying to get the ballerina back.*)

Scene Eighteen

(SUZY *and* ALLEGRA *in a car.* ALLEGRA *is driving.*)

SUZY. He goes, "What do you do?" and so I go, "I do anything."

ALLEGRA. *(subdued)* That's funny.

SUZY. You should have seen his face.

ALLEGRA. I'm sure.

(a long silence)

SUZY. You want to hear something funny?

ALLEGRA. What?

SUZY. I never told my mom we were borrowing her car.

ALLEGRA. You what!!?

SUZY. Relax. She's so drunk she won't notice for a couple of days.

ALLEGRA. But what if she calls it in stolen? I don't want to go to jail.

SUZY. Relax. She won't figure it out. Anyway, she never remembers the license plate. She always asks me. She'll probably just think it's been repossessed.

ALLEGRA. What about you?

SUZY. She'll think I've been repossessed too.

ALLEGRA. As long as...

SUZY. If we get pulled over, I'll take the rap.

ALLEGRA. Oh. OK.

SUZY. Jesus. I know who not to ask if I decide to become a bank robber.

ALLEGRA. Sorry. I'm worthless. I suck. Maybe you should go on without me.

SUZY. Forget it.

ALLEGRA. You really want to become a bank robber?

SUZY. Anything just to not be boring.

ALLEGRA. You're not boring.

SUZY. You are, you dirty skank!

ALLEGRA. Whore!

SUZY. Slut!

ALLEGRA. Gonorrhea pus!

SUZY. Rectal wart!

ALLEGRA. Cum slop!

SUZY. Discharge!

ALLEGRA. This discharge is taking us to the Pacific Ocean!

Scene Nineteen

(Hospital for the Mentally Deranged.)

*(**JOE** sits in a chair in a straight jacket. Two **PATIENTS** in straight jackets sit on either side of **JOE**. They may overlap each other and **JOE**.)*

PATIENT 1. Get away from me. Don't touch me.

PATIENT 2. My brains is full of worms.

PATIENT 1. They say that he's insane. Do you believe it?

PATIENT 2. I do. Let's festoon him.

PATIENT 1. I'm too tired.

PATIENT 2. Me too. Too tired and full of worms.

*(**INTERN** comes and injects **JOE** with hypodermic.)*

JOE. They can lock you up for loving something beautiful.

PATIENT 2. I can't move.

JOE. It's wrong to take things and it's wrong sometimes to give things too.

*(**INTERN** injects **JOE** with another hypodermic.)*

PATIENT 1. It's my soul and I'll do what I want.

JOE. They lock you up for fighting or for not fighting or not eating all your peas or not sitting still or sitting too still.

*(**INTERN** injects **JOE** with another hypodermic.)*

PATIENT 2. I can't move my arms.

JOE. They lock you for caring too much, for holding your hands wrong or for asking questions or for not saying a word.

*(**INTERN** injects **JOE** with another hypodermic.)*

PATIENT 1. I won't say a word.

JOE. They come and they decide things; the staff wields their power like struck gongs. They are white and strong and they get what they want. Where is my plant? They won't let me fill anything here. You have a box and you need to fill it and they just don't understand that.

*(**INTERN** injects **JOE** with another hypodermic.)*

PATIENT 2. Shut up!

JOE. They won't let me have dancers. How can I fill anything without dancers? Where have all the ballerinas gone?

(*INTERN injects* JOE *with another hypodermic.*)

(*The* PATIENTS *get up and become* BALLERINAS. *They dance beautifully around* JOE. *The lights become strange. Perhaps there are unusual sounds.*)

(*INTERN injects* JOE *with another hypodermic.*)

BALLERINA 1. I am the one you think you see when you don't see anything.

(*ALLEGRA appears, pale. She dances with the ballerinas.*)

JOE. Allegra.

ALLEGRA. You're a bad bad boy. No wonder your mother, no wonder.

JOE. No.

BALLERINA 2. You're a bad bad bad bad boy. Under the covers no wonder your mother she never no wonder no wonder.

JOE. No.

(*INTERN injects* JOE *with another hypodermic.*)

BALLERINA 1. You're a bad bad bad bad boy. In sluver do whother key duther you number.

JOE. No.

ALLEGRA. A glubber doe slubber she dubber.

BALLERINA 1 & 2. Grubber do rubber yo mubber discober.

(*JOE begins to scream.*)

(*ALLEGRA disappears. Light return to normal.*)

INTERN. Calm down. Sleep. Sleep.

(*The* BALLERINAS *become* PATIENTS *again. They sit and fall asleep.*)

JOE. Ahhhhhhhhhh! Aahhhhhh! Ahhhh!

INTERN. Shut up!

(*INTERN slaps him.*)

Scene Twenty

(On the other side of the stage, the Diner. **MARCO** *and the* **WAITRESS** *sit together.)*

MARCO. It's not like going into insurance or human resources or accounting.

WAITRESS. Or waitressing.

MARCO. Right. Those jobs are for people with compunctions. Sucessful theft is all about being aware in a way you never have been before and some of this will come from adrenaline, some is cultivated and some can't be learned. If you're one of those people that can't learn it, if you don't move fast enough or can't turn your head far enough, you just shouldn't attempt it. Getting caught is no fun.

WAITRESS. Sure.

MARCO. Let's say you're the right kind of person. You'll do it a few times and you'll get good. You will say, "this is too easy. I must be missing something." You will feel like a God. But listen to me now. This is the most important thing I'm going to say. If you don't hear the music, do not proceed. If you do not hear the music do not proceed. There is no room for messy actions. If it can't be pretty, you shouldn't do it at all. Because that's when things go wrong. Does John Travolta dance without music? Does he get out on that floor? No he does not and neither should you.

WAITRESS. I see.

MARCO. But most of it is simply having the nerve to do what no one else would attempt.

WAITRESS. I'm not really gonna start stealing shit.

MARCO. I didn't think you would.

WAITRESS. So tell me, what is it you steal exactly?

MARCO. Whatever I want. *(pause)* When I was doing that. But I'm retired now. I don't do that anymore.

WAITRESS. What do you do now?

MARCO. Whatever I want.

Scene Twenty-One

(**ALLEGRA** *and* **SUZY** *in the car.*)

SUZY. I have to sleep in a bed tonight I don't care what you say.

ALLEGRA. Why don't you sleep in the back of the car again? You seem to like that.

SUZY. No. I need a bed. I need room service. I need a bathtub.

ALLEGRA. They'll want money up front.

SUZY. So?

ALLEGRA. How are we gonna buy gas to get back?

SUZY. Christ! You're so…

ALLEGRA. What?

SUZY. Nothing.

ALLEGRA. I'm sorry.

(*pause*)

SUZY. It's OK. (*beat*) We're really good friends now, huh?

ALLEGRA. Yeah.

SUZY. Like best friends?

ALLEGRA. Uh huh.

SUZY. Best friends could stab each other and it'd be OK. We'd forgive each other for things, huh?

ALLEGRA. You mean like for stealing this car and not telling me?

SUZY. Yeah. That. And for kissing your boyfriend?

ALLEGRA. …

SUZY. Now you're mad.

ALLEGRA. …

SUZY. I didn't mean to. It just happened.

ALLEGRA. …

SUZY. I'm sorry. You deserve better anyway.

ALLEGRA. No I don't.

SUZY. Oh, honey, yes you do. We both do.

ALLEGRA. I think this trip was a mistake.

SUZY. No it wasn't.

ALLEGRA. Don't talk to me. Just don't talk to me.

SUZY. What did I do?

Scene Twenty-Two

(The Hospital. **JOE** *is in the same place. The* **BALLE-RINAS** *are around him about to put on a show. They release him from his straight jacket and face the audience. They perform a ballet as they tell his story.)*

BALLERINA 1 & 2. The Story of Joe.

BALLERINA 1. When Joe was born –

*(***BALLERINA 1** *changes her dress slightly to become* **JOE'S MOTHER.***)*

BALLERINA 2. His mother said –

BALLERINA 1. I don't understand him.

BALLERINA 2. She said –

BALLERINA 1. He's not like other kids.

BALLERINA 2. She said –

BALLERINA 1. He's not like my family. We should send him off far away to be with people like him.

BALLERINA 2. But Joe's Father said –

JOE'S FATHER. *(entering)* I see myself in him or what I could have been or what I would have been but am not. I don't understand him but I will take care of him and he can work in the shop with me.

*(***JOE** *tinkers in a corner with a machine.* **JOE'S FATHER** *watches.)*

BALLERINA 2. Joe's father owned a small engine repair shop and Joe still in diapers rebuilt engines without being taught how.

BALLERINA 1. People began bringing in objects that were not small engines for Joe to fix. Joe's father's business boomed.

BALLERINA 2. He changed the name to –

JOE'S FATHER. Small Engine and Appliance and Electronics and Computer and Clock and Watch and Car and Assorted Machine Repair Shop.

BALLERINA 1. For those customers who wanted to tip Joe for his hard work, Joe's Father instituted a policy of asking for wrenches instead of cash.

JOE'S FATHER. He doesn't understand money.

BALLERINA 2. *(as customer)* Joe, you did a great job on the dehumidifier. It's like new.

JOE'S FATHER. Sorry, he doesn't talk while he works.

BALLERINA 2. That's all right. Give him this, though, will you?

> *(***BALLERINA 2*** *hands* **JOE'S FATHER** *a wrench.*
> **BALLERINAS** *or other actors disguised switch off as* **CUS-**
> **TOMERS**. *They hand* **JOE'S FATHER** *wrenches which he*
> *piles around* **JOE***.)*

CUSTOMER 1. *(offering a wrench)* Thank him for fixing my scooter.

CUSTOMER 2. *(offering a wrench)* I thought I was gonna have to buy a new one.

CUSTOMER 3. *(offering a wrench)* He's quite spectacular.

CUSTOMER 4. *(offering a wrench)* You must be so proud.

CUSTOMER 1. Thank him.

CUSTOMER 2. Thank him.

CUSTOMER 3. Thank him.

CUSTOMER 4. Thank him.

BALLERINA 1. And then one morning, falling face-first on his plate of eggs over easy, at the age of fifty-three, Joe's Father had a heart attack and died.

> *(As* **JOE'S FATHER** *lies down, a large number of wrenches*
> *fall from the ceiling and clang to the ground. It rains a*
> *torrent of wrenches.* **JOE** *watches them fall.)*

BALLERINA 2. Joe's Mother couldn't look at Joe anymore. It hurt too much. He was too much like his father. So she sent him away to people, she thought, who could better take care of him. She packed his ballet videos and his clothing. She said goodbye to Joe, and two tears fell down alternate sides of her face as she kissed his cheek.

(BALLERINAS kiss JOE on the cheeks.)

BALLERINA 1. The wrenches remain in piles in Joe's Mother's basement. She never goes down there. Whenever anything in the house breaks, which is frequently, she buys a new blender or washer or clock or computer. She's a perfect consumer.

BALLERINA 2. But now and then, late at night she thinks of Joe and wonders how he is.

BALLERINA 1. When Joe came to the group home, he took an empty box as his own. Sometimes when he misses his wrenches or the repair shop or something else he can't explain, he has to put something in the box just to stop thinking. And when he has it in his possession, he's all right again for a few minutes or a few hours.

BALLERINA 2. Or at least he was before they took him away.

(The BALLERINAS put JOE back into a straight jacket and sit him down again. JOE wails.)

JOE. Aaaaaaaaahhhhh!

Scene Twenty-Three

(The Diner.)

(The **WAITRESS** *is sitting with* **MARCO**.*)*

WAITRESS. But to answer your question, I always wanted to be a detective. You know, like a detective?

MARCO. So you can catch thieves? Like Nancy Drew?

WAITRESS. Sure or Sherlock Holmes.

MARCO. May I ask why?

WAITRESS. Cause I'm good at discovering people's secrets.

MARCO. You know my secrets?

WAITRESS. I get people. I see things. I know things.

MARCO. What kind of things?

WAITRESS. Well, for example my husband. I knew he was on his way out. For weeks I smelled another woman in the way he showered her off, saw it in his eyes the first day and knew he wasn't going to stick around. Not that I knew what to do about it. But I knew he was going to leave. So it wasn't a surprise when it happened.

MARCO. Nothing's permanent, I guess. Even when we want it to be. People disappear.

WAITRESS. Other things too. I know who's gonna steal from the till. I know who's not gonna tip. I know you're spending an awfully long time in here.

MARCO. When do you get off?

WAITRESS. A couple hours.

MARCO. You wanna –

WAITRESS. What? Get some coffee?

MARCO. Or a drink.

WAITRESS. Yeah, all right.

MARCO. I think I'd like to retire here.

WAITRESS. Oh shit.

MARCO. You have a room to let? Or some space in your bed?

WAITRESS. Let's have a drink first.

MARCO. I'm just saying I'm thinking of settling down finally.

WAITRESS. And you're just going to proposition me cause I'm here.

MARCO. Not just cause you're here.

WAITRESS. What, you always wanted to fall in love with a waitress?

MARCO. I just know about you. I know you're good. Despite your detective tendencies.

WAITRESS. I know about you too.

MARCO. That bad, huh?

WAITRESS. Worse.

MARCO. Still, you want to have the drink.

WAITRESS. Gotta get to the bottom.

MARCO. I like the way that sounds.

WAITRESS. Fresh!

(**MARCO** *kisses her.*)

WAITRESS. Very fresh.

Scene Twenty-Four

*(Lights up on the **BALLERINAS**.)*

BALLERINA 1. In the dead of the night, in the heat of the desert, in the back of the car, in the land of strange dreams, Allegra sleeps.

*(The **BALLERINAS** dance. The dance ends. **ALLEGRA** arrives.)*

BALLERINA 2. *(to **ALLEGRA**)* You're on.

ALLEGRA. What?

BALLERINA 1. You're on. Quick. That was your cue.

ALLEGRA. I don't know what to do.

BALLERINA 2. You must dance. Do you want your father to be ashamed of you?

*(The music starts again and the **BALLERINAS** dance. They look at **ALLEGRA** expectantly.)*

*(**ALLEGRA** tries to dance but she has the steps wrong. She is off tempo. She leaps, she trips, she gets up again, trips again.)*

*(Meanwhile, **SUZY** and **BOBBY** are kissing. Then **SUZY** kisses **ALLEGRA'S FATHER**)*

SUZY. I can't decide who I like kissing better. Bobby or your father. They both like me better than you.

ALLEGRA. I hope you die! I hope you all die!

*(**BALLERINAS** start putting boxing gloves on **ALLEGRA**. **SUZY** continues to kiss **BOBBY** and **ALLEGRA'S FATHER**.)*

ALLEGRA. What are you doing?

BALLERINA 1. You have to fight.

ALLEGRA. Who?

BALLERINA 2. If you don't fight, your father will die.

*(**JOE** is wheeled out. He's still in a straightjacket and he's dazed.)*

BALLERINA 1. And it will be your fault because that's what you wanted.

BALLERINA 2. Go ahead.

BALLERINA 1. Hit him. If you don't hit him, your father will die.

JOE. Pretty.

BALLERINA 2. He's lying. Hit him.

ALLEGRA. You're lying.

JOE. You're pretty.

ALLEGRA. Liar!

    (**ALLEGRA** *hits him.*)

JOE. I'm very strong.

ALLEGRA. Killer!

    (**ALLEGRA** *hits him again.*)

JOE. Ow.

BALLERINA 2. What did you do?

BALLERINA 1. Stop hitting him. What did he do to you?

ALLEGRA. But you said.

BALLERINA 2. What a horrible little girl.

BALLERINA 1. Simply dreadful.

BALLERINA 2. How could you do that?

ALLEGRA. I'm sorry.

BALLERINA 1. No, you aren't.

    (**JOE** *gets up, takes off his straight jacket and hits* **ALLEGRA.** *She falls over.*)

ALLEGRA. I'm sorry. Stop. Help.

    (**JOE** *hits her again.*)

ALLEGRA. I'm sorry.

    (**BALLERINAS** *put her in the back of the "car."* **SUZY** *drives.*)

ALLEGRA. No! No! Stay away from me! Get away! I'm sorry. I'm sorry.

SUZY. Allegra! Allegra! Wake up! You're dreaming.

    (**ALLEGRA** *awakes.*)

Scene Twenty-Five

(The Diner. **MARCO** *kisses the* **WAITRESS**.*)*

MARCO. I like your lips.

WAITRESS. Thank you.

MARCO. And your eyes.

WAITRESS. Go on.

MARCO. And your nose.

WAITRESS. What else?

MARCO. I imagine you like all the wonderful things about me as well.

WAITRESS. You're full of yourself.

(**WAITRESS** *and* **MARCO** *kiss.)*

MARCO. Mmm. Minty. Let's get out of here.

WAITRESS. I guess I could close early.

(**SUZY** *and* **ALLEGRA** *enter.)*

SUZY. Hey.

WAITRESS. We're closed.

SUZY. You're shitting me.

ALLEGRA. Let's just go.

SUZY. I can't even get a cup of coffee? Have a heart.

(**WAITRESS** *looks at* **MARCO**.*)*

MARCO. I'm not in a hurry.

WAITRESS. Allright, but you have to make it quick and you have to get food.

(**ALLEGRA** *and* **SUZY** *sit and* **WAITRESS** *gives them menus.)*

SUZY. I'll have a cheeseburger.

WAITRESS. The grill's off.

SUZY. Well, what is there?

WAITRESS. You want a sandwich? Chips?

SUZY. Yeah. Give us whatever you got. And coffee.

(**WAITRESS** *disappears to kitchen.*)

ALLEGRA. *(whispering)* We don't have any money.

SUZY. Don't worry about it. I got it covered.

ALLEGRA. Don't...

SUZY. *(getting up)* I'll be right back.

ALLEGRA. I don't want to be here.

(**SUZY** *approaches* **MARCO.**)

SUZY. Hi there.

MARCO. Hello.

SUZY. I was wondering if you could help a girl out. You see me and my friend are a little down on our luck and I was thinking maybe you might like to buy us a meal. I'm not asking for money or nothing. Just a little food. I'll make it up to you.

MARCO. You will. How?

SUZY. Well, me and my friend are real good company. We're real good conversationalists.

MARCO. Conversation, huh?

SUZY. Sure. I'm Suzy.

MARCO. Marco.

SUZY. That's Allegra.

MARCO. Hi. Why don't you girls pull up a chair?

(**SUZY** *and* **ALLEGRA** *join* **MARCO** *at his table.*)

MARCO. So how old are you exactly?

SUZY. Why do you ask?

(**WAITRESS** *arrives with sandwiches and coffee and finds the girls have moved to* **MARCO**'s *table.*)

WAITRESS. Oh.

MARCO. We got to talking.

WAITRESS. Some sandwiches for the little girls and some coffee for the older man.

MARCO. Thanks.

SUZY. We'll have coffee too.

WAITRESS. Sure you wouldn't prefer some juice?

SUZY. Yeah I'm sure.

(**WAITRESS** *serves them.*)

ALLEGRA. So what's the name of this town?

WAITRESS. Why, you looking to buy a t-shirt?

SUZY. No thank you.

MARCO. These girls were just telling me about their travels.

WAITRESS. You're too young to be traveling by yourselves, aren't cha?

SUZY. No, we're not.

WAITRESS. You're not alone?

SUZY. We're not too young.

ALLEGRA. We're going to college in the fall.

WAITRESS. *(venom)* Good for you.

MARCO. I bet dessert would go real well with those sandwiches. Say, Lily, you got any cake or ice cream back there?

WAITRESS. We might.

MARCO. You girls like some dessert?

ALLEGRA. Yes, please.

WAITRESS. Eat your sandwiches first.

MARCO. Please, Lily.

SUZY. Yes, pleeease, Lily.

(**WAITRESS** *slowly heads towards the kitchen. Suddenly* **ALLEGRA** *stands up, stares out the "window."*)

SUZY. What?

ALLEGRA. Cops. Looking at our car.

WAITRESS. Tom don't like out of state plates.

(**WAITRESS** *exits into the kitchen*)

SUZY. Just chill out, OK. Just act cool.

ALLEGRA. What are we going to do?

MARCO. Is there a problem?

SUZY. We should be going.

MARCO. I see.

ALLEGRA. He's coming this way.

MARCO. I'm parked on the other side. You girls want a ride?

SUZY. Let's go.

ALLEGRA. I don't know.

SUZY. We'll come back for it tomorrow. If it's still here. What? You want to go to jail?

(**MARCO** *drops some bills on the table and leads them out of the Diner.* **WAITRESS** *comes out of the kitchen in time to see them heading for the door.*)

WAITRESS. Hey! Where you going?

MARCO. I'm just giving them a lift. I'll be back.

WAITRESS. Yeah?

MARCO. I'll meet up with you later.

WAITRESS. Well, I want to take a shower anyway.

MARCO. I'll be back in half an hour.

WAITRESS. Make it an hour at the Oyster.

MARCO. Wouldn't miss it.

(**MARCO** *kisses her and heads out the door after the girls.*)

WAITRESS. Don't be late!

(**MARCO** *leads* **ALLEGRA** *and* **SUZY** *into his motel room.*)

Scene Twenty-Six

(A bed or two. **MARCO***'s motel room.* **SUZY** *lies on the bed.* **ALLEGRA** *leans against the wall.* **MARCO** *is making them drinks at the table.)*

MARCO. You sure you girls want drinks?

SUZY. Make mine really strong.

MARCO. How bout you?

ALLEGRA. Just normal. Thanks.

MARCO. So how far did you drive that stolen car?

SUZY. It's my mother's.

MARCO. I'm not judging. I'm just asking.

ALLEGRA. We just decided to take a trip.

MARCO. You're lucky I happened to be around.

ALLEGRA. What do you do?

MARCO. I steal beautiful things and sell them. Or I used to. I'm retiring.

ALLEGRA. Like art?

MARCO. Sure.

ALLEGRA. I've never met someone like that.

MARCO. Maybe it's not the best line of work, but it calls to me, you know.

SUZY. I want to be an assassin.

MARCO. Ok.

SUZY. I do.

MARCO. You have a gun?

SUZY. They give you one when they train you.

MARCO. What about you? You want to be an assassin too?

ALLEGRA. I don't know what I'm doing.

MARCO. You're having a drink with me. *(They toast.)* To high crime and no punishment.

SUZY. To crime. So do you often lure young girls back to your room?

MARCO. Do you often go to the rooms of strange men?

ALLEGRA. I think I want to go home.

SUZY. Don't say that.

ALLEGRA. What are we doing out here? They're going to tow the car. We should go back.

SUZY. How we going to do that, Sherlock?

ALLEGRA. I don't know. It's just so stupid. What are we doing?

MARCO. It's not stupid.

SUZY. Of course not.

MARCO. You're feeling guilty, aren't you? Don't feel bad, girls. It's hard to be good all the time. Morality is for those who are afraid to try new things. Look what you did. You got in a car, drove all the way out here. At your age. Who could say they did that?

ALLEGRA. Yeah.

MARCO. Now you're in a warm dry place having a drink after having eaten a free meal. Sure you have no car, but you've got youth and beauty and a hell of a lot of spunk.

SUZY. Spunk?

MARCO. Makes me wish I was starting the game all over again. Makes me want to relive that first time I snatched that first little…I've had an illustrious career. But that first time…nothing comes close. I dunno. You think I should retire?

SUZY. Hell no.

MARCO. *(to* **ALLEGRA***)* What do you think?

Scene Twenty-Seven

(**WAITRESS** *in a spot. She talks to Tom, the police officer. We might see a silhouette of a policeman on a screen behind her.*)

WAITRESS. You have instincts and part of you knows things but the other part of you doesn't want it to be so. So you say, "no, that's not it." A does not lead to B because hey that's far fetched. Who would believe? The mind is being dramatic and should not be encouraged. Been letting it go too much. Too much time alone to consider too many possibilities.

But to answer your question, Tom, sure there was two girls in here. Had some sandwiches. Left right before you came in. Don't know where they went. Didn't say.

Just paid and left. Young girls. Too cute for their own good. Are they in trouble or are they themselves trouble? It's got to be one or the other. No, don't tell me. I don't need to know.

Can I offer you some ice cream? Sure, you can stay a minute. Or long enough for a bowl. Them girls is probably long gone by now. Down a back road never to be seen again. Now how 'bout that? Never to be seen again. That would be something.

Scene Twenty-Eight

(In the motel room, SUZY is asleep. ALLEGRA is talking with MARCO.)

ALLEGRA. She's out.

MARCO. You're not drinking.

ALLEGRA. I guess it was a long day. She's just tired.

MARCO. Don't you like the drink I made you?

ALLEGRA. I think she had too much of it.

MARCO. She talks too much. I thought we'd never be alone.

ALLEGRA. *(through nervous laughter)* I'm sure I could wake her up.

MARCO. You're afraid of me.

ALLEGRA. It's good you're here. I don't want to be alone. When I get alone I feel like I should run away. I think I'm a bad person.

MARCO. I'm also a bad person. It's best not to think about it. It helps if there are no consequences. It's an odd thing to live a life without consequences. I know I will never get caught. I'm really just too good. I'm uncatchable.

ALLEGRA. I'm not anything.

MARCO. I learned early that if something is pretty it must be wrong. Or it made me do things that were wrong which was the same thing. It's not my fault there is beauty everywhere.

Because when you look at something beautiful, it takes a little piece of your soul away. But you can't just let that happen. You have to do something. So you take the beautiful thing and run, because you think that will make you feel better but it doesn't help. It makes it worse somehow but what else can you do? You have to try to grasp it. You have to hold something like that in your hands. And when it takes from you, you have to take back. You can try to stop, but...Why aren't you drinking?

ALLEGRA. I don't want any more.

MARCO. I made it for you.

ALLEGRA. I don't think something's wrong just because it's pretty.

MARCO. *(coming up behind her)* Do you hear that?

ALLEGRA. What?

MARCO. The music.

> *(**MARCO** quickly covers **ALLEGRA***'s mouth and nose with a cloth. **ALLEGRA** struggles but then goes unconscious.)*
>
> *(**SUZY** falls off the bed suddenly.)*

Scene Twenty-Nine

(Still in the motel room. Both the girls are unconscious.
MARCO *is undressing them as he speaks.)*

(In a spot, **JOE** *in a straightjacket looks out at the audience.)*

MARCO. *(to* **ALLEGRA***)* Keep those beautiful eyes closed. Let
me look at you. Memorize you. Let me touch your skin
and breathe you in. Let me kiss the nape of your neck.
Isn't this better for you, without the complications of
having to react to my touch? Everything I do is what
you want. Tomorrow maybe I'll find a way to unload
you but now, well, now, you're mine, aren't you?

*(***MARCO*** *takes out a Polaroid camera and takes pictures.)*

JOE. Some people get locked up and some people never
do. If you try to kiss the staff they will lock you up.
It is illegal. Many men in suits never go to jail. That's
because that's because that's because they aren't me.
They aren't broken. They walk on the surface of the
water while everyone else is stuck in traffic or your
car breaks down. Their cars never break down. They
are super untouchable. They get married, they have
wives and children because they are men that are not
born broken. They are the people who are up on the
big screens. They are on the TV, on the radio, in the
newspaper because they are the chosen the good,
the other people. They can kiss whoever they want
or kill even. Even kill. Because they are uncatchable
or they are forgivable or they are perfect. They have
people lying to help them. Their mothers loved them
and told them so. Their mothers helped them up the
stairs. Their mothers had a lot of money and a lot of
good things in their bodies that they passed on while
they lived in their good homes. They were beautiful
and rich and were friends with all the people you are
supposed to be friends with. Like doctors who can lie

for you. Like doctors who can fix you. Except they don't need fixing. Not the super untouchable. They have legs like razors and eyes that magnetize. They are pretty. They are everything. Like Allegra. I wonder if Allegra is super untouchable.

MARCO. No need to move. You don't have to pose. You don't have to do anything. You're perfect just the way you are. Just let me remember you like this.

(**MARCO** *leans over and kisses* **ALLEGRA** *on the lips.*)

(**MARCO** *picks up his coat. Puts it down again…Kisses* **ALLEGRA** *again.*)

MARCO. No, I shouldn't. I shouldn't. But it just feels so right, doesn't it?

Scene Thirty

(*The Motel room.* **MARCO** *looks at the photographs he has taken. He lets them drop to the floor, puts his head in his hands.* **SUZY** *wakes up. She looks under the covers in the bed she shares with* **ALLEGRA**. *She sees they are not wearing any clothes or at least much less.*)

SUZY. Where are my clothes? Allegra, wake up.

ALLEGRA. What?

SUZY. Where are our clothes?

MARCO. They're here.

ALLEGRA. What did you do?

MARCO. I should have left an hour ago.

SUZY. Was there something in my drink?

MARCO. I don't make mistakes like this. I should have left already. I'm sorry. I guess I want to ask you if you'd like to come with me.

SUZY. I'm not going anywhere with you.

MARCO. Not you.

ALLEGRA. Get out! Get out!

MARCO. You sure?

(**ALLEGRA** *begins to hurl things at* **MARCO**. *Whatever she can find.* **MARCO** *doesn't even try to dodge the projectiles.*)

ALLEGRA. Get out! You fucker! I hope you die! I hope you rot and die! Fucker!

MARCO. But I think I love you.

ALLEGRA. Police!

MARCO. But –

ALLEGRA. Police!

(**MARCO** *exits.* **ALLEGRA** *throws a phone after him.*)

ALLEGRA. Fucker!

(**ALLEGRA** *covers herself in some way as she gets out of the bed.*)

ALLEGRA. Fucking asshole.

(*SUZY lies in bed, not moving.*)

SUZY. Did he...?

(*long pause*)

ALLEGRA. Yeah, I think he did. I don't remember...but, I think...

SUZY. (*Pause. Breaking down.*) What's wrong with me?

ALLEGRA. (*comforting her*) Nothing. Nothing. Don't cry.

SUZY. He saw me and he saw how ugly I was so he wouldn't touch me.

ALLEGRA. No, no honey. Shhh. It's OK.

SUZY. It's not OK.

ALLEGRA. It's OK.

(*ALLEGRA picks up pictures off the floor.*)

ALLEGRA. Look. Look how beautiful you are.

SUZY. No, you are.

ALLEGRA. You look really great.

SUZY. Yeah. We should burn these.

(*One by one SUZY and ALLEGRA take the photos and burn them in the hotel room trash can. There are a lot of photos and it takes some time. We can see the girls' faces shining from the firelight. It is solemn. Their movements are natural and then more graceful as if choreographed. The BALLERINAS may arrive surreptitiously and watch the fire over the girls' shoulders. When this scene has ended, the BALLERINAS take the trash can full of ashes into Scene Thirty-One. They dump the ashes into JOE's box and exit.*)

Scene Thirty-One

(Back at the Group Home, **ALLEGRA** *goes to see* **JOE.***)*

ALLEGRA. They told me they took you away and I'm sorry about that. I know that's my fault and I didn't mean for that to...I don't know what I meant – I just got out and it was better I guess or I thought it would be but then something bad happened and that was much worse. But you don't need to know about that. It's – You don't ever need to know about things like that.

Anyway, now my mom's mad at me because she had to fly out and get me but I think she's madder I didn't go to the funeral but I really came back to say I was sorry, which I am. I'm really sorry. I guess I just, I don't know. I was flying across the country just to get away but I just felt just as bad whenever I stopped and had to think. There's a lot of time to think out where there's nothing. You're probably angry at me.

JOE. They let you go.

ALLEGRA. Yeah.

JOE. They let me go too.

ALLEGRA. Yeah.

JOE. They ran out of money. Why'd they let you go?

ALLEGRA. I don't know.

JOE. OK. OK then.

ALLEGRA. You don't belong here, do you, Joe?

JOE. Where?

ALLEGRA. Maybe I could talk to Melody or something.

JOE. OK. I used to fix more things, Allegra.

ALLEGRA. You did, didn't you?

JOE. I'm quite independent.

ALLEGRA. You are, aren't you? Maybe if you were out on your own, I could see you on the weekends, but then maybe eventually I wouldn't come see you some weekend and then it would be two weekends in a row and then three and then maybe there would be someone my own age and we could talk about things and hear each other and I'd forget about you except when I wanted to feel guilty. We have now, though, don't we?

JOE. OK.

(ALLEGRA *kisses him.*)

JOE. No. No! Stop. Ahhhh! Ahh!

ALLEGRA. It's OK. It's OK. I'm sorry.

JOE. Don't. Ahh! Do. Ahh! That.

ALLEGRA. It's OK. I don't work here anymore.

JOE. OK. I don't think you should do that. I don't think you should do that, Allegra.

ALLEGRA. I'm sorry. I won't do that again.

(JOE *looks in his box.*)

JOE. OK. They're trying to prevent this facility from becoming sexualized. I appreciate your cooperation.

ALLEGRA. What are you talking about?

JOE. …

ALLEGRA. Joe, what do you mean?

JOE. There are no more ballerinas, no more kissing the staff.

ALLEGRA. Did they take your ballet videos away?

JOE. Yes.

ALLEGRA. I'm sorry, Joe.

JOE. OK.

ALLEGRA. What if I danced? I used to be a ballerina.

JOE. You were a ballerina.

ALLEGRA. I'm going to dance for you.

JOE. OK.

ALLEGRA. I'm a pretty ballerina.

JOE. Pretty.

(ALLEGRA *begins a few tentative steps. She gets into it.* JOE *looks away, looks back again, looks away ashamed.*)

ALLEGRA. Look at me. It's not wrong. It's not wrong.

(**JOE** *looks again.* **ALLEGRA** *continues her dance. Her dancing lures the other* **BALLERINAS** *out. It's as if she has brought them back. The* **BALLERINAS** *join her, doing more complicated versions of* **ALLEGRA***'s dance. The* **REST OF THE CAST** *may dance as well. Their dance is full of joy.*)

End of Play